LIFE OF ST. AETHELWOLD

Wulfstan the Cantor

Translated by: D.P. Curtin

Dalcassian
Publishing
Company

PHILADELPHIA, PA

ISBN: 979-8-8692-1250-4 (Paperback)

Library of Congress Control Number:
Author: Curtin, D.P. (1985-)

Printed by Ingram Content Group, 1 Ingram Blvd, La Vergne, Tennessee

First printing edition 2012.

THE LIFE OF ST. ETHELWOLD

The preface begins.

On the life of the glorious Father Aethelwold the bishop, whose sacred memory is celebrated on the Kalends of Augustus, on which day the heavenly kingdom departed.

After Christ, the Savior of the world, appeared to the human race incarnate through the hall of the virginal womb, and having completed the ineffable dispensation of his piety and our salvation, he returned to the seat of the paternal majesty with the triumph of glory. let the darkness escape from the hearts of men, and in order to inflame the minds of the believers with the fire of heavenly love, and quench the hunger of prolonged begging, and satisfy the multitudes of peoples with the food of eternal life. From whose college the blessed father and chosen priest of God, Aethelwold, appeared in his times, like a lucifer shining among the stars, the founder of many convents and the instituter of ecclesiastical dogmas, he alone shone singularly among all the English priests. Of whose birth, deeds, and death, we thought it worthy to narrate something to those who wished to know, and lest the memory of such a great Father should be consigned to complete oblivion; It will be useful to us who have written, and to those who are going to read or hear it.

BEGIN THE CHAPTERS OF THE NEXT BOOK.

I. Of the rise and times of the blessed Bishop Aethelwold.

II. About the vision of his mother's dreams.

III. On the interpretation of the same dreams.

IV. How the mother felt that the child's soul had come to be born, and that it had entered into him. one day he was found suddenly in the church with his nurse.

V. How a child was born and reborn in Christ, in a certain way

VI. How diligently and diligently in his childhood he devoted himself to the study of sacred literature

VII. How, as a young man, the effect known to King Adelstanus reached the clergy and the priesthood.

VIII. Of the prophecy which Saint Aelphegus, bishop of Winton, foretold concerning the three priests.

IX. How Aethelwold arrived at Glestonia, and became a monk, and how he lived there.

X. Of the death of King Aethelstan, and of the succession of his brothers to the kingdom of the English nation.

XI. How, in the favor of King Edred, the holy man took charge of the Abbandun monastery, and was ordained abbot of that place.

XII. That King Eadred came to the monastery, and the guests, who had been feasting all day, could not drain the liquor.

XIII. That in the reign of Eadgar the temple of the aforesaid convent had been built and dedicated.

XIV. Of the ordination of Dunstan, and that the abbot Aethelwold directed the monk Osgarus across the sea; and about a certain brother of Aelstan, a man of simple and great obedience. He tried to put out the chance of a certain post.

XXXIX. Concerning the vision of the man of God, in which there appeared to him a very large ship, filled from bottom to top with fishes and eels, which were awakened and became men, and were restored to their former order.

XL. Of the new dedication of the old church, which took place on the 13th day of the month of November.

XLI. On the death of the holy father in Cal. of Augustus, and of his burial on the third day of the ninth of the same month.

XLII. How the holy man, before he was raised from the tomb, manifested himself to a certain urban man, named Ethelmus, who had been punished with great blindness.

XLIII. Of the transfer of the holy man, which took place on the 4th day of the Idus September, and of the miracles performed at his tomb.

XLIV. Of the weak girl who was healed there.

XLV. About the blind boy, who himself was enlightened there.

XLVI. Of a certain thief bound and stretched out in prison, who was freed by the word of the man of God alone.

THE LIFE OF SAINT AETHELWOLD, BISHOP AND CONFESSOR OF WINTON, BEGINS.

CHAPTER I.--The parents of the holy priest Aethelwold were, therefore, descended from a pure Christian branch, of the city of Wentana, flourishing in the time of Edward the Elder, king of the English, faithfully walking in the commandments and justifications of the Lord without complaint. Those who, while increasing their daily good works, were adorned by the extraordinary gift of God, by which they deserved to beget such a child, by whose education and examples not only the people of the present age, but also of the future, would come to the knowledge of the true light: that, stripped of the dark darkness of error, they would enjoy the glory of eternal brightness.

CHAPTER II.--And so his happy mother, when she was carrying him conceived in her womb, saw a dream of this kind on a stormy night, which was a sure foreshadowing of future results. For it appeared to him that he was sitting before the doors of his house, and that there was before his blinds a kind of lofty standard, the top of which seemed to touch the sky: which, bowing honorably to the earth, he surrounded the pregnant woman with the veil of his fringes, and again raised to a lofty height, and strong in inflexible stability, whence he himself the sky bowed down. But when the woman awoke, she again sank into slumber, and behold, suddenly she saw leaping from her mouth and flying like a golden eagle of wonderful size, which, in its flight, overshadowed the buildings of the city of Wentana, with its golden wings, and disappeared in the height of the heavens. And when the woman, waking up, was astonished with herself, and the vision of the dreams rolled over in silence in her mind, and could not by herself guess their interpretation, she went to a certain servant of Christ, named Aetheldrida, mature in character and age, who was in the aforesaid city a nurse of the virgins devoted to God, to whom she told from the order which had been shown to him in a nocturnal vision. But she, as she was very wise with a shrewd mind, and sometimes also of the future, revealing to the Lord, foreseeing, foretold many things about the unborn child, which indicated that the outcome of things was true.

CHAPTER III.-- We too can be the dreamers of the same dreams, understanding in the sublime standard the holy man who was then carried in the womb, sometimes the future standard-bearer of the army of God, as he was, whom we saw coming together with many kinds of reluctance against the ancient enemy for the defense of the holy mother Church, and himself fighting, nay, conquering through God himself, we saw the devices of the wicked reduced to nothing. And because the eagle is called from the corner of his eyes, and by witnessing the sacred speech a desirable treasure rests in the mouth of the wise; rightly by the golden eagle, which was seen to overshadow the whole city with a veil of wings, the same illustrious man is represented adorned with the [treasure] of all wisdom; who, meditating on the divine line of a perceptive and unreverberating heart, always flew to the heavenly things through contemplation, and over the Church, the city of the great King, which the opposing powers strove to attack, spread far and wide the shelter of the paternal protection, and, having completed the course of the good struggle, arrived at the vision of God in the company of the saints , as it is said in the Gospel in the voice of Sunday: Wherever the body is, there the eagles will gather. Because where our Redeemer himself is in the body, there is no doubt that the souls of the elect are now gathered there, and in the glory of the future resurrection their bodies will also be gathered there. We have said this briefly about the interpretation of dreams: now let us return to the order of the narrative.

CHAPTER IV.--For on a certain day when his mother was standing in the church packed with citizens, desiring to attend the celebration of the sacred mass, she felt the soul of the child she was carrying in her womb come, and entered into him by the nod of God who controls all things, just as afterwards the saint himself who was about to be born, already the bishop reported to us with joy. From which it is shown that he was chosen by God even before he was born, and that the soul of a procreated man does not, as some estimate, take the beginning of existence from the father or from the mother, but, as is truly and without all doubt believed, to be quickened by the vital spirit from the Creator alone, and in detail to be given to each The future priest of God was born, and reborn at the fountain of baptism in Christ.

CHAPTER V.--For it happened on a certain solemn day, when, as usual, his nurse had decided to go to the church and devote herself to prayer, so strong a storm of inundating rain broke out that she could not move a foot outside the threshold of the place, where she was sitting holding the same child in her lap. While she was mourning and wept most bitterly, because she could not fulfill her vow of pious devotion, she bowed her head humbly to the Almighty Lord, and at once was comforted by divine mercy. For feeling no discomfort from the tempestuous storm, she was suddenly found with the child sitting in the church which she had planned to go to, where the priest was celebrating the solemnities of the masses: and as she could not have believed with any reason that it would happen, she was greatly frightened by the fact; and all who were aware of this miracle were overcome with astonishment of great astonishment. For just as the prophet was once suddenly taken from Judea, and deposited in Chaldea with a meal, so the blessed boy Aethelwold was presented in a moment with his nurse in the temple, so that just as he revived the prophet Daniel in the lion's den at the appropriate time, so he would feed thousands of people in the church of the saints.

CHAPTER VI.--Therefore, with daily progress, the boy grew up with a good character, and in his early childhood was given over to the sacred studies of literature: so that he who was to show others the way of salvation, should himself sit humbly with Mary at the Lord's feet, and hear the word healthily from his mouth. For he was of an agile nature and of a keen intellect, so that whatever he had learned by the tradition of his elders, he did not pass it over lazily to oblivion, but rather committed it to a tenacious memory. He strove also to overcome the tender years of his childhood by the honesty of his manners and the maturity of his virtues, to enslave all his members in divine obedience always, and to direct the whole intention of his mind to the fulfillment of God's will.

CHAPTER VII.-- And when he had reached the age of flourishing youth, the tidings of his holy conduct to King Aedelstan, the son of the aforesaid King Edward, were told by popular report, and he ordered the young man to be hastily approached, who, when brought to stand in the presence of the king, found favor in his sight and in the eyes of the nobles his and there, spending a great deal of time in the palace with an individual company, he learned many useful and profitable things from the wise men of the king. And finally, at the command of the king, by Aelphegus, bishop of Winton, according to ecclesiastical custom, he was first circumcised to the clerical office, and then, after a few passing years, he was consecrated to the priestly rank.

CHAPTER VIII.-- For Father Aelfegus himself of blessed memory, among the other gifts of spiritual charisms bestowed upon him, was influenced by the spirit of prophecy, and it happened that he ordained at the same time Dunstan and Aethelwold, and a certain one, by the name of Aethelstan, who, afterwards abandoning the monastic habit, continued as an apostate in Venice. At the completion of the celebration of the mass, Saint Aelfegus addresses the antists adhering to him thus: of the English; but the other will sometimes succeed me to the dignity of a priest, and the third will melt away in a pitiful end through the flattery of lustful pleasures. Then Aethelstan questioned his relative, the holy antichrist, saying: "Will it happen to me that I am one of the two who are to be exalted to the episcopal chair?" To whom the ancients answered: "You will have no part or lot in the order I have mentioned before; but you are not going to continue in that sanctity, which you seemed to have begun in the sight of men. The event proved how truthfully the words of whose prophecy had been uttered. For two (as the Scripture says: The just shall be justified yet, and the holy shall be sanctified yet) reached the honor of the pontificate, while the third, in accordance with the terrible threat of the previous sentence which says: He who is in filth, let him be filthy still, ended his life in the stench of luxury.

CHAPTER IX.-- But Aethelwold, a servant of Christ, benevolent in name, mind, and work, treading the narrow path that leads to life in the right way, he daily cooperated with God and strove to grow in improvement, paying careful attention to the teachings and examples of Elfegus, his undertaker and organizer. For he remained for some time with the king commanding him, in order that he might be better imbued with him; Having made much progress in his teaching, he at last took from him the habit of the monastic order and devoted himself with humble devotion to his government. For there he learned the liberal skill of the art of grammar, and the sweet sweetness of metrical reason; and after the fashion of the wisest bee, which is wont to seek out the trees of a good smell by flying round, and to lean upon the vegetables of a pleasant taste, she plucked the flowers of the divine scrolls. He also diligently read the Catholics and the named authors, moreover he perseveringly insisted on vigils and prayers, and exercising self-control, and always exhorting his brethren to the arduous task. When he was loved by all for the merit of sanctity, and was appointed dean of the monastery by his abbot; he ran into no danger of exaltation, but he set an example of humility to so many subjects, that he labored daily with the work of his hands in cultivating the garden, and prepared for his brethren apples and vegetables of various kinds for lunch: that after the spiritual refreshment of souls, he also ministered to the needs of bodies, always keeping before his eyes that of Dominic: Whoever if he wishes to become greater among you, let him be your servant; and he who wills to be first among you shall be your servant; and that: How great you are, humble yourself in all things, and you will find grace before God. Commending these and other testimonies of the Scriptures to memory, he guarded his subjects with discipline and by humility.

CHAPTER X.-- Meanwhile it happened that the most victorious king
Aethelstan, in the fourth year after he had destroyed the hostile army of the
pagans with great slaughter, died, and his brother Eadmund took the helm of
the kingdom in his stead. Six and a half years after he was cruelly murdered, his
brother Eadred succeeded to the kingdom, who was a special lover and
defender of the old convent in Winton, as evidenced by the ornaments which
were made at his command, namely, a large golden cross, a golden altar, and
other things which his generous hand he directed thither to the honor of the
blessed apostles Peter and Paul, and ordered them to be preserved there
eternally to the praise and glory of God: who, even if his life should become a
count, arranged to adorn the eastern portico of the same Winton church with
gilded roofs. In the time of whose reign the Lord Aethelwold, still desiring to be
taught a greater knowledge of the Scriptures, and to be more perfectly
informed in the monastic religion, resolved to go beyond the seas. But the
venerable queen Eadgiw, the mother of the said king, prevented his attempts,
giving advice to the king not to allow such a man to leave his kingdom,
asserting, moreover, that there was such wisdom of God in him, that it might
be sufficient both for himself and for others, although for this reason he had to
go to the borders of a foreign country it would not tend at all.

CHAPTER XI.-- The king, pleased with what he had heard, began to have a
great love for the servant of God, and it pleased him, persuading his mother, to
give to the holy man a certain place called Abbandus, in which there had
formerly been a little monastery, but at that time it was neglected and desolate,
consisting of mean buildings, and possessing only forty estates; but the rest of
the land of the aforesaid place, which revolves from one side to the other by a
hundred cansadas, was possessed by the king himself, subject to the royal
dominion. And it was done, with the consent of Dunstan the abbot, according
to the king's will, that Aethelwold, the man of God, should undertake the care
of the place foreordained, in so far as he might ordain therein monks regularly
serving God. The servant of God therefore came to the place entrusted to him:
he was immediately followed by certain clerics from Gleston, namely Osgarus,

Friwegarus Foldbirthus, and Ordbirthus of Winton, and Eadricus of Lundonia, submitting themselves to his discipleship. And he gathered to himself in a short space a flock of monks, whom he himself ordained as abbot at the command of the king. The king also gave the royal property which he had possessed in Abandonia, that is, a hundred castles with the best buildings, to the abbot and brothers for the increase of their daily subsistence, and he helped them a great deal in money from his royal treasury. but his mother directed more generous consolation gifts to them. And the Lord brought so much grace to his servants, that to the aforesaid convent, which was formerly very poor in things, all the riches were supposed to flow together, and thus all things met with good success, so that the promise of Dominic's sentence was clearly seen to be fulfilled, in which it is said: Seek first the kingdom of God and his justice. and all things shall be added unto you.

CHAPTER XII.--Therefore the king came one day to the monastery, that he might direct the structure of the buildings by himself; and he measured all the foundations of the monastery with his own hand, just as he had decided to erect the walls, and asked the abbot to dine with his people in the guest house. The king nodded at once, and it happened that there were not a few of his nobles present, coming from the tribe of the Nordanhimbri, who all went to the feast with the king. And the king rejoiced, and ordered mead to be poured out abundantly to the guests, the doors being carefully closed, lest anyone should be seen to leave the drinking of the royal feast by fleeing. What a lot? The servants drank liquor all day long to the satisfaction of the guests; but he himself was unable to drain the liquid from the vessel, except to the measure of a palm, in the drunkenness at the suggestion of Nordanmbria, and in the evening they retired with rejoicing.

CHAPTER XIII.-- However, Aethelwold the abbot did not begin to build the work designated for him in the days of King Eadred, because the same king quickly departed from this life on the 9th of the month of December. But during the reign of the glorious King Eadgar, the distinguished and most merciful, the most powerful and invincible son of King Edmund, he built and finished in the same place an honorable temple in honor of the holy Mother of God and the ever-virgin Mary, which to this day is shown better by sight than by word.

CHAPTER XIV.--About these times Abbot Dunstanus was elected to the episcopate of the Church of Wigorn, according to the prophecy of the bishop of St. Elfegus, as we touched upon above. And after a career of some years, he became an archbishop, and remained at Kent for thirty-seven years, like an immovable pillar, foremost in doctrine and action, beautiful with an angelic countenance, preeminent in alms and prophecy: at whose tomb we have often heard heavenly miracles performed. And Aethelwold sent the monk Oscar across the sea to the monastery of Saint Father Benedict of Floriacense, that he might learn there the manners of regular respect, and by teaching the brethren at home to show how far he himself followed the rule of the monastic religion, and together with his subjects turned away from every deviance, the flock entrusted to him to the promised land of the heavenly kingdom would lead In which congregation there was a certain brother named Elfstanus, a simple man and a man of great obedience, whom the abbot ordered to provide for the victuals of the artisans of the monastery, to whose service he submitted himself most devoutly, he cooked meat every day, and diligently ministered to the workmen, kindling the fire and bringing water, and again of his own accord cleaning, thinking that the abbot would do this with the consolation and help of another minister. For it happened one day, while the abbot was passing through the monastery as usual, that he looked at that brother near the boiling cauldron, in which he was preparing food for the artisans, and as he entered he saw all the vessels very clean, and the floor swept, and said to him with a cheerful face: O my brother Elfstane, this obedience You have stolen from me, which you practice without knowing me. But if you are such a soldier of Christ, as you show yourself to be, put your hand into the boiling water, and forcefully draw one piece from the bottom for me, who immediately, without delay, putting his hand to the bottom of the cauldron, drew out a hot piece, not feeling the heat of the boiling water. When he saw this, the abbot ordered that the piece be laid down, and that no one living should be told of this. But we saw that brother afterwards ordained an abbot, who was also afterwards exalted to the pontifical honor, was prefect of the church of Wiltun, and finished with a blessed end in the Lord.

CHAPTER XV.-- For Saint Aethelwold was a great builder of churches and other works, both while he was abbot and while he was bishop. Hence the common adversary lays upon him the usual plots of his malice, in order to exterminate him, if he could by any means. For one day, while the man of God was working on a structure, a huge post fell on him and threw him into a certain pit, breaking almost all his ribs on one side, so that unless the pit had received him, he would have been completely crushed.

CHAPTER XVI.-- The holy man, however, recovered from this trouble, by the adjutant grace of God Almighty, and Eadgar, the most fortunate of the English, elected him to the episcopate of the church of Winton, before the church was dedicated to the aforesaid convent. And by the command of the king, Dunstanus, the archbishop of the Church of Doroburn, consecrated it, in the ninety-sixty-third year of Sunday's incarnation, under the third day of the calendar of December, on the vigil of St. Andrew the Apostle, which was then held on Sunday, the first Advent of our Lord and Savior Jesus Christ. And there were then in the old monastery, where the pontifical seat is held, canons involved in evil habits of crime, being prevented by elation and insolence and lust, so much so that some of them deigned to celebrate masses in their order, putting away the wives they had unlawfully married, and taking others, and continually giving themselves over to gluttony and drunkenness. The holy man Aethelwold, not bearing this in the least, having been given permission by King Eadgar, expelled the detestable blasphemers of God from the monastery as soon as possible; and bringing monks from Abbandonia, he settled there, of whom he himself was abbot and bishop.

CHAPTER XVII.-- And it happened on Saturday, at the beginning of Lent, while the monks coming from Abandonia were standing at the entrance of the church, that the clerics were finishing the mass. Singing communion: Serve the Lord in fear, and rejoice in him with trembling; take hold of discipline, lest you should stray from the just path, as if they were saying: We do not want to serve God, nor to keep his discipline; When the brothers heard this, they rejoiced, understanding that their journey had been successful from the Lord, and that this psalm had been sung because of their presence, and soon they drew the Davidic command to themselves, Osgar exhorting them and saying: Why are we tarrying outside? Let us do as the canons exhort us, let us enter, and marching along the path of justice, serve our Lord our God with fear and exultation, so that when his anger flares up in a short time, we may deserve to be partakers of those about whom it is subjoined: Blessed are all who trust in him.

CHAPTER XVIII.--The king also sent there with the bishop one of the most famous of his ministers, whose name was Wulfstan Aetdelham, who, by royal authority, ordered the canons to choose one of two things, either to give place to monks without delay, or to assume the habit of a monastic order. But they, overcome with great terror, and cursing the monastic life, immediately went out as the monks entered; but still afterwards three of them came to conversion, viz. Eadsinus, Vulsinus, and Wilstanus the presbyter. Those who had left the convent, which they had left behind when they had been expelled, returning with a humble heart, submitted their necks to the yoke of Christ. For until now at that time there were no monks in the nation of the English, except only those who stayed in Gleston and Abbandonia.

CHAPTER XIX.--Afterwards, when the aforesaid brothers had begun to keep the norm of a regular life in the old convent, and there many old people, converted to the ministry of God, young people brought, and little children flocked there; out of the envy of the clerics it was given to the bishop to drink poison in his court while dining with his guests, and to show them all humanity, insomuch that, having extinguished it, they would drive out the servants of God, and being gathered together again could freely enjoy their former debaucheries. For he was dying immediately after three or four mouthfuls of a little something to drink: and he drank, not knowing that all the poison that was in the cup had been brought to him, and immediately his face became pale, and his bowels were tormented by the excessive force of the poison. But he hardly got up from the table, going to the bed, and spread the poison through all his limbs, already threatening himself with immediate death. But he at last, reflecting, began to reproach himself, and said to his mind: Where is your faith? Where are the thoughts of your senses? Are not the words of Christ true and faithful, which he promises in the Gospel, saying: And if the believers drink anything deadly, it will not harm them? Is not he who speaks these things present to the divinity, though absent from the body? Undoubtedly, He, who is always able to do everything, can empty this poisonous virus into you. Faith kindled in him by these and such words, he extinguished all the lethargic drink he had drunk, and rising furiously, driven away by the pain of the poison, he went to the hall with a cheerful countenance, showing no signs of pallor at all to those who were looking at him, nor returning any evil to his sorcerer, but forgiving him what he had done wrong. Thus, by the power of God, the evil plan of the clerics was dispelled, who, seeing that their wickedness could not prevail, dispersed hither and thither through the different provinces of the English nation, until they ended their lives.

CHAPTER XX.-- From that time the eagle of Christ, Aethelwold, the ancients, spread his golden wings, and with the nod of King Eadgar, he drove the canons out of the New Monastery, and there he introduced the monks, conversing regularly. And Edelgar, his disciple, ordained for them an abbot, who afterwards became bishop of the province of the southern Saxons, and after Saint Dunstan's transfer to the heavenly realms, became archpriest of Canterbury.

CHAPTER XXI.--In Abbandonia, however, he established Osgarus as an abbot, and that place was enriched with six hundred and more than that, supported by privileges, moreover, of eternal freedom, written down by divine and royal authority at the same time, which, sealed with gold plates, are preserved there to this day.

CHAPTER XXII.-- In the third convent of Winton, which is called Nunnamenster in English, consecrated to God in honor of the ever-virgin Mary, he organized the herds of holy nuns, whose mother, of whom we have touched a little above, Etheldrida, presided over them, where the rule of regular life has been observed until now.

CHAPTER XXIII.-- Not only in the borders of the Western Saxons, but also in remote parts of Britain, the holy ancestor Aethelwold took care to gather monks to the service of God Almighty. For there is a certain famous region situated in the province of the eastern Angles, surrounded by marshes and waters in the manner of an island, whence it received the name Elige from the abundance of eels which are caught in the same marshes. In which region the place is considered worthy of all veneration, magnified, of course, by the relics and miracles of the holy Queen Etheldrida and the perpetual virgin and her sisters; but at the same time, he was despondent and committed to the royal treasury. This place, therefore, the servant of Christ, because of the love of so many virgins, began to be greatly venerated, and at a price of no small sum of money, he bought it from King Eadgar, establishing in it no small flock of monks. To them he appointed the abbot of Brithnodus as his superior, and he renewed the site of the same place in the most decent manner with monastic buildings, and commended it to the Almighty Lord, richly enriched with the possessions of the world, and strengthened by the privilege of eternal freedom.

CHAPTER XXIV.--He also obtained another place in the region of the Girvii at a price from the king and the nobles of the land, situated on the bank of the river Nen, to which the English language once imposed the name of Medeshamstede, but is now commonly called Burh. The basilica of which place, adorned with suitable structures of houses, and abundantly enriched with the adjacent lands, he consecrated in honor of the blessed Peter, prince of the apostles, and there in like manner assembled a group of monks. But Ealdulf, his monk, was appointed abbot over them, who, after the death of Lord Oswald, assumed the archbishopric of the Church of Eburacensis. The third, nevertheless, he acquired for a price, a place situated near the bank of the aforesaid river, which, on account of the brambles and growths around it, called Thornig by the usual English name, which he delegated as the most suitable for the monks on equal terms. He also appointed a rector and abbot Godeman in charge of them, and built a monastery in honor of Mary, the mother of God and the virgin Mary, and blessedly enriched him with the possession of all goods.

CHAPTER XXV.-- Now Aethelwold, a man of God, was magnificently powerful in the words and works of the famous King Edgar, dedicating churches in most places, and everywhere preaching the Gospel of Christ, according to the admonition of the prophet Isaiah, who said: "Shout, do not cease, lift up your voice like a trumpet, and declare to my people their iniquities, and to the house of Jacob their sins.

CHAPTER XXVI.--Whose preaching was most aided by the holy antitus Suvithunus, who at the same time was revealed by heavenly signs, and was most gloriously transferred below the royal temple, and most decently placed. And therefore, in the house of God the twin luminaries shine together, with golden candlesticks superimposed upon them: for what Aethelwold preached with salutary words of exhortation, this Suvithunus wondrously decorated with a glorious exhibition of miracles to the praise of the name of Christ.

CHAPTER XXVII.--Thus it was done, with the consent of the king, that partly by the counsel and action of Dunstan, partly by the diligent co-operation of Aethelwold, monasteries were established everywhere in the English nation, some for monks, some for Sanctimonials, under abbots and abbesses living regularly. And Aethelwold, the servant of Christ, went round every monastery, instituting manners, admonishing the obedient with words to advance in good, and severely correcting the fools to depart from evil with lashes.

CHAPTER XXVIII.--For he was terrible as a lion of the unlearned and perverse; but to the humble and obedient he presented himself as a very gentle lamb, so moderating the severity of serpentine prudence that he did not lose the gentleness of the simplicity of a dove. Whom if ever the zeal of rectitude would compel him to impose the laws of discipline upon his subjects; The fury itself did not proceed from cruelty, but from love; and inwardly he loved with paternal piety those whom he chastised outwardly as if he were following him. He was the father and shepherd of the monks, the vigilance manager of the holy nuns and the protector of the virgins; the comforter of widows, the host of strangers, the defender of the churches, the corrector of the wandering, the refresher of the poor, the helper of orphans and orphans; which he fulfilled more by work than our smallness can develop by speech.

CHAPTER XXIX.--For it happened at a certain time, that a bitter famine oppressed the whole country of Britain violently, and the greatness of the want extinguished most of them with a terrible defeat. But the Lord's man, having compassion on the multitude of those who were afflicted with hunger, spent every portion of the money which he had for the use of the poor. And when the money failed, he ordered the ornaments and most of the silver vessels to be taken from the treasures of the church, and he ordered them to be broken into pieces and reduced to money. He thus protested with the deepest sigh of his heart, that he could not equanimously bear that dumb metals should last whole, while man, created in the image of God, and redeemed by the precious blood of Christ, should perish in beggary and hunger. Having bought food, he supported an innumerable multitude of the needy, who, desiring to escape the danger of starvation, had taken refuge to him from all sides, and those who lay destitute in the streets and in the streets, destitute of all comfort, he relieved by feeding them, rescuing the wretched from the very jaws of death, and also providing daily food to each: until mercy God would look down from heaven to earth, and by helping the human race with his usual piety, he would control the evil of poverty. In whose work of piety, he followed the imitable example of the blessed Lawrence the Levite and martyr, who, in a time of urgent persecution, scattered the treasures and resources of the Church and gave them to the poor, so that his justice might remain for ever and ever, and his horn might be exalted in glory.

CHAPTER XXX.-- It is true that the Lord, as the Scripture says, chastises whom he loves, and scourges every son whom he receives; The man of God was frequently weakened in the bowels, and suffered from a swelling disease in his legs. He usually spent sleepless nights because of the pain; and by day, although he was pale, he walked as if he were healthy and felt no discomfort, remembering the apostolic consolation in which it is said that virtue is perfected in weakness, and again: For when I am weak, then I am stronger and more powerful, and again: I will gladly glory in my infirmities, so that the power of Christ dwells in me. And although he was struck with a sharp pain, he never used the meat of four-footed animals or fowls, except once, when he was compelled by the greatest sickness for three months: (which he did by the order of Archbishop Dunstan) and again in the sickness of which he died.

CHAPTER XXXI.--For it was always sweet for him to teach youths and youths, and to give them Latin books in English, and to give them the rules of grammatical art and metrical reasoning, and to exhort them to better things with amusing speeches. Hence it happened that many of his disciples became priests and abbots, and honorable bishops, and some even archbishops in the English nation.

CHAPTER XXXII.-- Among these things it pleased Almighty God, that even the heavenly sign should be shown, that it pleased him to dwell in his holy place. For when the ancients were making a certain sacred journey, in order to sow the seed of God's word in Dominic's field; it happened that his cleric, to whom the holy chrism had been appointed, had received less oil than was necessary, and this little that he had received on the journey itself to have lost And when the servant of Christ had arrived at the appointed place, after the celebration of the mass, and after the sweet discourses of the holy preaching, he commanded, as was the custom, that oil should be presented to him for strengthening the children. But the clerk, who had thought to carry the ampoule with him, suddenly recognized that he had lost it. Disturbed, therefore, he quickly resumed his journey from whence he had come, and carefully looking around here and there, he found a bottle of chrism lying in the road full of oil, half of which indeed a little before he had had some liquid. Having assumed this, he returned with great fear and joy, satisfying the holy ancient, and spreading the miracle of the heavenly drops with a truthful report. This is proved to have been done by the nod of God, as he was filled with the grace of the Holy Spirit, and by his anointing the hearts and faces of many rejoiced; he himself would be rewarded not only inwardly, but also outwardly with the oil of heavenly joy.

CHAPTER XXXIII.--There was a certain monk living under his mastership, who, with a demonic instinct, committed the crime of theft. Wherefore the whole assembly was overcome with great sadness, while each subject thought that he was being treated by another brother, which he knew without a doubt that he had not done. For which matter the holy elders in the meeting of the brethren ordered a modest rebuke, that if anyone was aware of the theft, he should return the thing he had stolen as soon as possible with the blessing of God or throw it in such a place where it could be found. But that brother hardened himself with a stubborn heart and neglected to keep the commandment of the man of God. After three days and three nights had passed, when the stolen thing had by no means been found, the holy man spoke in the chapter before all the multitude of the brethren, saying with terrible indignation and threat: "That sacrilegious man would not return the money which he had stolen with a blessing as we had commanded; let him return it only with the curse of Almighty God, and let him himself be bound not only in soul, but also in body by our authority. What a lot? said the brothers: Amen. And behold, that monk was sitting invisibly bound, his arms clinging to each other under his hood, and he remained stupid, thinking what he should do. All the rest of his limbs, however, were movable and fit for use, with the exception of his arms, which the holy man, by the authority conferred upon him by God, bound and rendered useless. At last, when the chapter was over, he arose, the poor man thus bound, and going out behind the holy bishop confessed to him secretly that he had been guilty, and that he had committed the crime of robbery; yet telling him nothing of the bond by which he was bound. But the bishop, seeing him seized with great terror, as it was his custom to forgive those who repented and cried, and to condole with the bowels of compassion, answered in a gentle speech: "You have done well at least, though by confessing your sin too late: you may now have our blessing." And at once his arms were loosed, unbeknownst to the bishop. But he, coming out of thence, was exceedingly glad, and told by order of his binding and release to a certain brother named Wulfgar, who advised him that this should be kept more in silence, and that it should be revealed at a suitable time afterwards. From this fact it is given to be understood, of whose merit this man was before the Lord, who, though unaware, showed so much prowess by speech alone. For because he guarded the pastoral care of the holy government with faith and morals worthily, he certainly obtained the turn of the blessed Peter, prince of the apostles, by binding and loosing.

CHAPTER XXXIV.--Therefore, when the man of God had determined to renew the old church with great effort, he commanded the brethren to insist frequently on the labors together with the craftsmen and workmen, with whom, working in competition, the work of the building grew gradually in the sublime, supported on this side by numerous oratories, in which the votes of the saints were faithfully venerated by all will benefit those who approach. It happened one day, while the brothers were standing on the top of the temple with the masons, that one of them, named Godus, fell from the top to the ground. As soon as he reached the ground, he rose up and stood unharmed, suffering no harm from such a fall. And in the sight of all who were present, he went up to the place where he had previously stood; and taking the trowel, he continued more diligently at the work which he had begun. To whom, then, is this miracle to be ascribed, but to him, at whose command he went out to do the work of obedience? who therefore could not be harmed, because he bore the merit of a man of God in his case and protected him safe from the danger of falling.

CHAPTER XXXV.--At a certain time of winter, when the brothers, according to the edict of the rule, would rise earlier for vigils (*Rule of St. Benedict, chapter 2*), and in the night interval they would serve in psalmody and reading; a certain monk, named Theodricus, went to the man of God, wanting to inform him of a certain necessity, and found him holding a candlestick of light in his hand and reading, and with the diligent agility of his eyelids sharpening blinded old men: and he stood there for a long time, paying attention as he intently fixed his eyes on the page. At length the holy man arose from his reading, and that brother who was sitting took the candle, and began to read, proving whether he too could sharpen his healthy eyes to read as diligently as he had seen the bishop make his blind men. But that recklessness did not go unpunished by him. For on the following night, when he had given his limbs to sleep, a certain unknown man appeared to him, with a terrible threat, saying to him: "With what rashness did you presume to reproach the bishop last night in the reading?" And when, trembling, he denied that he had done this, he glared at him with the lights: "You cannot, said he, play at deceiving me, as you think: but this is a sign of your presumption." And saying these things, he struck a blow violently at his eyes with his finger, and a strong pain in his eyes immediately followed, which afflicted him violently for many days, until by satisfaction he blotted out the fault which he had carelessly committed against the holy man.

CHAPTER XXXVI.--It also happened that when Christ's servant was attending to his reading at night, he fell asleep because of excessive vigilance, and a burning candle fell from the candlestick onto the book in which he was reading. She lay burning on the leaf for a long time, until one brother, named Leofred, arrived. He hastily took the still-flaming candle from the book and looked at the sparks of the candle lying along the many lines and blowing them out found the page unharmed. In this matter the merit of the holy man was evident, because the burning candle was consumed by the flame, and he lost so much of his strength as not to injure the page.

CHAPTER XXXVII.--These things we have given to Christ in brief, that we may incite both present and future, and all the faithful to love and respect the humble devotion of such a great Father. Moreover, it is not easy for us to explain how much or what kind of dangers Saint Aethelwold endured for the defense of the monks, or with what kind affection he loved the studious and obedient brothers, or how much he worked on the structure of the monastery by repairing the church and building other houses; or how vigilant he was in his prayers, and how devoutly he exhorted the brethren to the remedy of confession, or how many thousands of souls he took from the devil, and brought them to heaven, having been given to God. But from these few things may be known, which cannot be told by us.

CHAPTER XXXVIII.--For it was necessary to fulfill the dream which Saint Dunstan, that glorious and angelic archbishop of the English nation, had once seen of him. For when he was abbot of the monastery of Gleston, and under his rule the servant of Almighty God Aethelwod, as we have said above, saw in his dreams, standing outside the dormitory, as it were a tree of wonderful height, which seemed to spread its branches to the east and west, north and south, over extending over the whole country of Britain in vast length and breadth. The branches of whose tree were innumerable were laden with greater and smaller hoods, but the tree itself at its top wore one very large hood, which towered over the others with a veil of sleeves, and, rising above them all, reached the sky itself. But the Lord's man, Dunstanus, greatly astonished at such a vision, asked these things of the presbyter, who showed him an angelic dog and was decorated, saying: "Please, venerable elder, what is this strong and lofty tree, whose branches spread far and wide are seen to support so innumerable hoods." To whom he answered: "This tree which you see, Abbot Dunstan, marks the position of this island; and the great hood which is erected on the top of this tree is that of your monk Aethelwold, who is devoted to Christ in this monastery; but the rest of the hoods, with which these branches seem to be laden, denote a multitude of monks, who are to be instructed by his learning, and to be gathered from every part of this region to the service of Almighty God; and under his leadership they will reach the glory of the kingdom of heaven, and the fellowship of the blessed spirits reigning with Christ. When he had received this answer, the holy man awoke, silently considering the vision with himself, and afterwards telling it to the faithful in a faithful report. In the course of time, the popular report became known to many people, and at last it came to the knowledge of our littleness as well.

CHAPTER XXXIX.--Neither the less nor the other thing was necessary to fulfill the dream which the holy man of God Aethelwold himself related to us at one time, saying: "I thought that I was standing near the shore of the sea, where it seemed to me that there was a certain great ship, in which there was a great multitude of fish, and most of the eels were kept closed from the bottom to the top. And when I was silently thinking with myself, what this dream which I saw meant, suddenly I heard a voice calling me by my name, and saying to me: Aethelwold, Aethelwold, this is a command from heaven sent to you by God. Arouse these fish with which this ship which you see is filled, and by your prayers cause them to be men, as they were before. At whose command I immediately obeyed, stood for them to pray, and, drenched in a shower of tears, groaning, I said: Lord Jesus, to whom nothing is impossible, look more mercifully on the souls deceived by diabolical trickery, which are alienated from the sense of human reason, and in beastly fashion in this slippery they are pitifully involved in the chaos of the age. Please, good Jesus, do not allow the enemy of the human race to triumph over them, but through the omnipotence of your holy name they will be resurrected to life, so that, escaping the dream of eternal death, they will know you as the true and only Savior of the world, and henceforth always to the calm harbor of your salvation that they may take refuge, be free from all the perturbations of the world, and remain safe under your government. For it is yours, O Christ, to give life to the dead, and to restore your image, which you have created, to its original beauty, who came into this world to save sinners, and who suffered the terrible tortures of death on the cross, deigned to shed your precious blood for the salvation of us all. When I poured out these and similar words of prayer with a contrite heart and a spirit of humility, behold, those whom before I had seen fish wrapped in the mire of dung and in the lake of misery, suddenly I see men made and raised from the dead. I had specially recognized many of them: among whom one, falling backwards, turned again into an eel, that is to say Aethelstan, who had once been ordained a priest with me, whom I could not afterwards raise in any way, nor make him become a man. The rest, however, all unanimously raised their voice to heaven, clapping their hands, and giving thanks to Almighty God, because by his ineffable mercy and by the advent of my littleness they deserved to be recalled from death to life, and to be restored to the human reason which they had lost. But I wake up rejoicing in the Lord, and congratulating them, and this vision to you, O my little one! therefore I report that you too may persevere in the holy purpose with the worship of good works, whereby, by the grace of God, you may be numbered among those who, though unworthily, have been committed to me, that they may be saved gladly from the sedulous abyss of this world and in eternal bliss without end. These dreams which we have noted were indeed seen at that time: but from that time to this day they do not cease to be fulfilled, while everyone, fervent with divine love, hastens to leave the world and lead a cloistered life; and as long as the common people strive to turn away from evil, and to do good, and humbly submit their necks to the King of kings, to Christ: inasmuch as both monks and laymen, following the footsteps of the holy Father Aethelwold, deserve the eternal joys of attaining the heavenly kingdom.

CHAPTER XL.-- In the ninety-eightieth year of the incarnation of Dominic, the church of the old convent was renewed and built, nine priests dedicating it solemnly and with great glory; the presence of King Aethelred, and in the assembly of almost all the dukes, abbots, counts, and first nobles of the entire English nation, who celebrated the dedication with all joy the same two days: about which we also congratulating in the Lord, we sang this song: Prince Aethelwold full of holy breath. He performed many works pleasing to God. This ancient man also repaired the courts of the temple with high walls and new roofs. Strengthening this on the parts of the South and on the parts of the North, with solid arches and various arches. He also added several sacred houses with altars, which keep the entrance to the threshold of doubt. Whosoever, as if unacquainted, walks through the halls of these plants, he does not know where he is going, and where he is to set his foot. Because the doors are seen open on every side, and no sure path of the road is clear to him. Here and there the wanderers standing round the birds, Attica covered with mazes and amazed by the sun. He came more assuredly until he had a guide, and he led him to the last threshold of the gate. At this, wondering with himself, he consigns himself to the cross, and cannot know whence he departs with his astonished breast. Thus built, the machine that supports the old church flashes, and so does the variegated twinkling. How that pious Father, filled with the greatest piety, To the praise of the Celsitonous name Yesterday He supported, covered, endowed, and consecrated it, and deserved to pay his vows in the temple, In the present modest face of King Aethelred, On the throne of the kingdom that remains today. There the priests were present, singing three times, completing the holy service. The first of these was Dunstan, mature in appearance and actually snowing with gray hair and angelic. The lucifer of the English, Lord Aethelwold, benevolent in heart, stands by this company. After seven others, whose names are here written in verse with a dactylic foot. Elfstan, Edelgarus, and again Aelfstanus, and Aeswig Aelfeh, Edelsinus, and here was Aethulfus. And finally, on the tenth cup, the bishop came there, doing no work, drinking many cups. After the others there were many nobles and leaders, the greater part of the Gentiles and the English. Whom he had gathered together from the council. That which had been the village of the king in Andeveran, the same shepherd singing and often singing Aethelwold, As the Lord's grace had given him. And all celebrate the greatest solemnities of the temple, Applauding the Lord with a bosom of praise. And let them rejoice over the good things, that kind one above all, who decreed that the prince should be given riches to all, Dishes are allowed to eat, all food is plentiful, No one is present sad, all are present cheerful. There is no hunger, where all are full of food, and the table remains full of food. Butlers and vagrants often frequent the cellars and ask the guests to start drinking. They set the bowls, and crown the sweet wines, Mixing drinks with innumerable drinks. And so, day after day went forth in hymns, And all hearts blessed God. At last, they had all finished solemnly with hymns, which the voice of the people rang out in honor of God. Every one of them returned to the shores with joy, rejoicing in the Lord with their chests and singing with their mouths. There was never such a dedication of the temple, I think, in the whole nation of the English, as was the Wenta celebrated powerfully in the city In the old monastery of St. Peter. That the almighty God thus protects the immaculate, that this may be a shelter worthy of him. And whosoever lowly enter this asylum Shall rejoice in the full share of pardon.

We thought it would be appropriate to insert it here after publishing this about the renewal and dedication of the Old Church. From then on, divine piety brought such grace to the holy priest, that those sublime rulers of worldly powers, leaders, tyrants, and judges, and all who had hitherto seemed to oppose him and oppose him in the way of God, suddenly became like sheep from wolves, and worshiped him with a wonderful affection. and bowing their necks to his knees, humbly kissing his right hand, men of God should commend themselves in all things by their prayers.

CHAPTER XLI.--At the same time when the holy ancestor Aethelwold was about to depart from this mortal life, and to receive the rewards of his labors from God, he came to a town called by its common name Beaddingtun, sixty miles distant from the city of Winchester. When, therefore, he had tarried there for some time, he began to be burdened with acute infirmity; and having been anointed with the liquid of the sacred oil, he secured his departure by the perception of the body and blood of Dominic. Having thus said farewell, and giving peace to his sons, between the words of a prayer he returned his spirit to heaven on the Kalends of Augustus, in the ninety and eighty-fourth year of Dominic's incarnation, and in the twenty-second of his episcopate, with Aethelred king of the English ruling the kingdom. Those who were present there testified to us that, on examination, the body of the holy man was renewed by a sudden change, permeated with a milky whiteness, and beautiful with a rosy blush, so that in a way it seemed to present the face of a seven-year-old boy, in whom already a certain glory of the resurrection appeared through the display of the changed flesh. But it is impossible to tell how many people assembled for his funeral. The rich and the poor flocked together from the neighboring towns and forts to say their last farewell to their shepherd. All followed the coffin with sorrow and bitterness of heart, with an incomparably precious treasure, armed with the most holy Gospels and crosses, adorned with veils of mantles, lit with lights and heavenly hymns, and fenced on this side with concerts of psalms. On the following day, when they entered Winton to meet the body, the whole city met with one accord. From here you could see crowds of monks cheering; thence pale trains of maidens; from here you could hear the voices of the clerics singing on high; hence the groaning of the weeping poor, and the howling of the crying needy, who could not bear to be deprived of the presence of their Shepherd, gave infinite cries of tears to heaven. The man of God was then brought with the heavenly funeral to the church of the blessed apostles Peter and Paul to his episcopal seat, and after the vigils and solemn masses, he was buried in the crypt on the south side of the holy altar, where he should rest, as he himself reported to you, once he had been shown to heaven it is.

CHAPTER XLII.-- In the twelfth year after the death of the glorious priest Aethelwold, it pleased the heavenly dispensation to reveal him by heavenly signs, and to lift his bones from the bulwarks of the sepulcher, so that the lamp which had been hidden for a time under the lamp, was placed on the candelabrum, so that it might give light to all who are in the house. For there is a certain small city, abounding in commerce, which is commonly called Weallingaford, in which there dwelt a certain vigorous man, whose name was Elehelmus, who, losing the light of his eyes by an accident, suffered blindness for many years. Saint Aethelwold of Gallicin stood before him in his dreams, and warned him to go to Winton early, and approach his tomb to receive grace, saying: because I must be lifted from the grave in which I lie. He who heard these things and recognized the voice of the one speaking with him, thanked the holy Father for deigning to visit him; and because he was completely ignorant of where he was buried, how he could have known his tomb and gone to it, he diligently inquired. when you have entered, cause a certain Wlesfan monk, surnamed Cantor, to come to you. When he hears the words of my message from your mouth, he will undoubtedly lead you to my tomb, everywhere you will receive the light of your eyes. » Who much? That credulous man, following the words and promises of the holy priest, hastened to Wintonia, entered the church, approached the aforesaid brother, and demanded that he fulfill the mass of the blessed Father, telling him and all who were present the order of the vision. For it was the evening in which the birth of Mary, the most sacred mother of God and the perpetual virgin, is solemnly and worthily celebrated throughout the world. But that brother, wondering, placed himself midway between hope and fear, and humbly obeying the commands of the holy priest with a close foot of obedience, led the blind man to the cave of the sarcophagus, who remained there all night in prayer, and in the morning no longer needing a guide, returned with joy to his own he is a seer, blessing the Lord with his heart and mind.

CHAPTER XLIII.--This revelation was spread far and wide, which had been confirmed by such an evident miracle. Thenceforth the servant of Christ appeared manifestly to the said brother Wulfstan, and to most others by a night vision, and revealed to them by these and these signs, that it was pleasing to the will of heaven that he should be removed from the tomb and placed worthily in the church. Therefore, the venerable priest Elpheagus, his successor, with a shrewd mind, going through such things with him, returned the humblest thanks with an eager heart to the almighty Christ, because he had deigned in his time to amaze his saint with heavenly signs. Nor tarry; gathered together by the brethren of the clergy, and the multitude of the people, he transferred the relics of the holy prince Aethelwold with honor on the fourth day of September and placed them in the choir of the church; We looked at the information.

CHAPTER XLIV.--There was at that time in the city of Wentana a certain little girl, the daughter of a certain Adelwardian householder, who was very weak, and was tortured almost to the point of death. This being led by his mother to the tomb of the man of God, he fell asleep a little. Awaking immediately, he got up in good health, and returned home with his mother rejoicing.

CHAPTER XLV.--A certain little boy, the son of a certain meek and modest man of Aelfin, was deprived of light in his very infancy, and led by his mother's arms to the grave of the venerable Father Aethelwold. With a wonderful saying, soon the mist of blindness was removed, and the coming brightness of the light opened the eyes of the child, all the people rejoicing, and faithfully giving thanks with all devotion to Christ, who can do all things.

CHAPTER XLVI.-- Nor is it to be passed over in silence that the aforesaid successor of the holy man, Elfagus the Antistes, ordered a certain thief, who had been scourged for multiple crimes, to be sent to the prison to be tortured with more severe punishments. And when he had lain thus condemned for a long time in punishment, one night the holy priest Aethelwoldus came to him in a vision and said to him: "Wretched man, why do you lie stretched out on the stake for so long? But he, recognizing the holy man, whom he had often seen in mortal life, answered: "You deserve, my lord, I bear the punishments, and I am thus tormented by the just judgment of the bishop, because I have been frequently caught in thefts, and I have not ceased from them; but I repeated the evils I had done again and again. Then the saint: "Cease," said he, "or at least the wretched one, cease from theft, and be freed from the bond of this fetter." "The wretched man arose at once, freed, and coming out of thence, fell at the feet of the bishop Aelpheagis, and told him the matter that had been done around him in order, and he, for the honor of his great Father, allowed him to go away unscathed. It is therefore agreed that this saint, united to eternal life by the power of his merits, is able to release us from the bonds of our sins and lead us to the heavenly kingdoms, to whom the power of binding and loosing has been granted still in the flesh of the heavenly one who dwells in the flesh, by the excellency of our Lord Jesus Christ, who with God the Father, coeternal, and by the Holy Spirit God lives and reigns, for endless ages of ages. Amen Begins the hymn in honor of St. Aethelwold's forefathers with an elegiac and paraethereal poem composed through the alphabet,

Prince Aethelwold is ministering light to the people; the candle is shining. This warrior of God has fought victorious battles, this warrior of God rushes into arms. From whose sacred mouth flowed the dogmas of life, we have received every good from whose sacred mouth. Let us sing songs to the Father with a sweet and pious heart; let us sing songs with a sweet and pious heart. Behold, your pontifical pinnacle shines abundantly. Here and there your pinnacle shines. The source and source of good ran through you sowing words, In you the source and source of good flowed. Your glory will be eternal now, and therefore throughout the age that you meritoriously retain, the glory will endure. With the love of this flock you despised the spikes of death, driving the strong ones from here with the love of this flock. Eadgar, the mighty and mighty king, fell in love with thee. Let the camp of God rebuke thee and let the camp of God rebuke the honeys of David. The monastic crowd applauds you with countless praises and rejoices with you with countless praises. The lofty walls of your house had lifted this man's care, you celebrated the sacred hymn of the breast night and day, paying the sacred duty night and day. You scattered the seeds of light in all these places, you drove out the darkness in all these places. Be vigilant, we ask, defender of students. Keep watch over your protective servants. Whatever is harmful, cut off; Bring back what is good, and cut off what is harmful. Happy apostolic director and janitor of this court and apostolic director of the Church, Loose your servants in Peter's turn, loose those who are bound, Loose us from our sins your servants. Guided by thee, let us climb as the halls of heaven, partakers of the kingdom, guide thee, leded by the stars. We sing these songs with hymnic verses, and we worship you Patronus with hymnic verses. Because you used to multiply Christlike souls, recalling Christlike souls to the heavens. Let the offending hydra flee, lest it play us by the wayside: Let your right hand cover us, let the offending hydra flee. Jealousy cannot be restrained, since Christ overcomes the evil one: Christ is present as the conqueror, jealousy cannot be restrained. Look, Holy Father, at what adversities tire us: at what evils tear us apart, look, holy Father. May those who serve as students be gentle with you. Those who praise you, be gentle with you. Rescue, shepherd, the sheep, with your heart that you have always loved, and rescue, shepherd, the sheep that you have nursed. Mark our names as Christ marks our names in the fortress of the Poles with his saints. Amen. The vespernal hymn was published in Sapphic metre, containing Adonius in the fourth place.

The humble shepherd and ruler of the people, whose glorious triumph we venerate, Now Aethelwold reigns in the stars, happy without end.

Who was our Father and teacher, Exhibiting the sacred documents of life, and always endeavoring to please God with a kind heart.

O holy day, famous, shining, Which the piety of God has consecrated for us, that we may so much deserve the song of Merere alms!

Now let us ask him with every effort, that he may wash away our pious guilt, and lead us by his holy prayer to the high Olympus.

To God alone be glory and power, Praise in the highest, honor and everlasting, who rules the whole world by His laws. Amen. Honorable senator of heaven, holy Father of the Church Aethelwold, hear your supplications, servants. Already a star among the stars, shining above the ether, obtains for us the charisms of the kind Paraclete. We beseech you with our minds bowed down here before your arms, be present to our prayers serene and propitious. That, protected by your necessary protections, we may reach the eternal joys of the heavens, the only begotten, Holy of both Spirits, triune and one Lord, provide for us. Amen.

The Scriptorium Project is the work of a small group of lay people of various apostolic churches who are interested in the preservation, transmission, and translation of the works of the early and medieval church. Our efforts are to make the works of the church fathers accessible to anyone who might have an interest in Christian antiquities and the theological, philosophical, and moral writings that have become the bedrock of Western Civilization.

To-date, our releases have pulled from the Greek, Syriac, Georgian, Latin, Celtic, Ethiopian, and Coptic traditions of Christianity, and have been pulled from sundry local traditions and languages.

Other Selections from the Early Anglo-Saxon Church Series:

Life of St. Edmund by St. Abbo of Fleury (Nov. 2005)

Church Laws by Alfred the Great, King of Anglo-Saxons (May 2006)

Church Laws by Guthram, King of East Anglia (Feb. 2007)

Two Works by St. Dunstan of Canterbury (Jan. 2008)

Life of St. Dunstan by Byrhtferth of Ramsey (Mar. 2008)

Canons to Wilfinus by St. Aelfric of Abingdon (Feb. 2009)

Life of St. Aethelwold by Wulfstanthe Cantor (Sept. 2012)

The Eight Principal Vices by St. Aldheim of Malmesbury (May 2013)

For the Catholic Easter and the Roman Tonsure by Ceolfridus of Wiremouth (June 2013)

Penitential (Poenitentiale) by Theodore of Tarsus (July 2013)

Life of St. Augustine of Canterbury by Goscelin of Saint-Bertin (Aug. 2013)

Laws & Charters by Edgar, King of the English (Mar. 2015)

The English Calendar by St. Bede the Venerable (Nov. 2015)

Letter to King Aethelred by Pope John VII (Dec. 2015)

The Life of the Christian by Fastidius of Britain (Apr. 2017)

Privileges of the Abbot of Canterbury by St. Augustine of Canterbury (Sept. 2017)

A Song of Aethelwolf by Aethelwolf of Lindisfarne (Nov. 2017)

Decrees of Aethelbert by St. Aethelbert, King of Kent (Feb. 2019)

Donations by St. Aethelbert, King of Kent (May 2020)

Life of St. Augustine of Canterbury by Goscelin of Saint-Bertin (Dec. 2020)

Canons of the Council of London by Edgar, King of the English (Dec. 2023)

www.ingramcontent.com/pod-product-compliance
Ingram Content Group UK Ltd.
Pitfield, Milton Keynes, MK11 3LW, UK
UKHW021448130125
4077UKWH00044B/1293